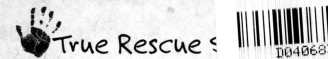

True Rescue S

True Underground
Rescue Stories

Jeff C. Young

Enslow Publishers, Inc.
40 Industrial Road
Box 398
Berkeley Heights, NJ 07922
USA
http://www.enslow.com

To my cousin, Jane Ellen Johnson

Library of Congress Cataloging-in-Publication Data

Young, Jeff C., 1948-
    True underground rescue stories / Jeff C. Young.
        p. cm. — (True rescue stories)
    Summary: "Readers can learn about the rescues of Jessica McClure, Floyd
Collins, the Quecreek Mine Rescue, the Elandsrand Mine Rescue, and Wesley
Autrey"—Provided by publisher.
    Includes bibliographical references and index.
    ISBN 978-0-7660-3676-5
    1. Rescue work—Juvenile literature. I. Title.
    HV553.Y68 2011
    363.34'810922—dc22

                        2009049675

Printed in the United States of America
082010 Lake Book Manufacturing, Inc., Melrose Park, IL

10 9 8 7 6 5 4 3 2 1 *4621 2063 6/11*

To Our Readers: We have done our best to make sure all Internet addresses in this
book were active and appropriate when we went to press. However, the author and the
Publisher have no control over, and assume no liability for, the material available on
those Internet sites or on other Web sites they may link to. Any comments or sugges-
tions can be sent by e-mail to comments@enslow.com or to the address on the back
cover.

♻ Enslow Publishers, Inc., is committed to printing our books on recycled paper. The
paper in every book contains 10% to 30% post-consumer waste (PCW). The cover
board on the outside of each book contains 100% PCW. Our goal is to do our part to
help young people and the environment too!

Photo Credits: Shutterstock.com

Cover Illustration: Shutterstock.com

Contents

Underground Rescues Facts

Jessica McClure

The well that "Baby Jessica" fell in was 120-feet deep. Fortunately, she only fell about 22 feet before being wedged between rocks.

Jessica McClure's rescue was front-page news in more than just the United States. It was also the lead story in Japan and many European countries.

Midland, Texas, was home to McClure, as well as many other famous people. Among them are actors Woody Harrelson, Tommy Lee Jones, and Kathy Baker.

Floyd Collins

Floyd Collins was an experienced caver by the time he was a teenager.

Sand Cave, where Collins was trapped, is now part of Mammoth Cave National Park in Kentucky.

The National Guard had to be called in to maintain order once Collins was trapped and his attempted rescue became a media frenzy.

Quecreek Mine Rescue

The Quecreek Mine was located in Lincoln Township, part of Somerset County in southeastern Pennsylvania.

Rescue crews used a GPS (global positioning system) to figure out the exact location of the trapped Quecreek miners. Many people think of a GPS as something they have in their cars or as a feature on their cell phones, but GPS systems are also a fantastic tool for search and rescue teams.

Despite the risks of coal mining, the United States continues to mine more coal than any country other than China.

Elandsrand Mine Rescue

The Elandsrand Mine is also known as the Elandskraal Mine.

According to a press release from the Harmony Gold Mining Company, forty-eight days of production were lost due to the mining disaster.

Fortunately, all 3,200 miners trapped at Elandsrand survived the accident.

Wesley Autrey

Wesley Autrey was enjoying time off of his construction job with his two daughters when he was thrust into the spotlight after saving the life of Cameron Hollopeter.

Autrey was given a standing ovation after being singled out as an example of a courageous American by President George W. Bush during Bush's 2007 State of the Union Address.

According to the New York Transit Museum, as of 2010 the New York subway system serves nearly 5 million riders per day.

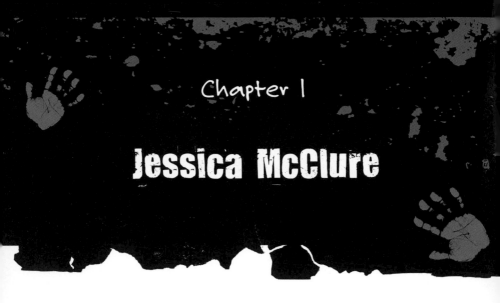

Chapter 1

Jessica McClure

J essica McClure was a curious eighteen-month-old toddler with a near fatal attraction to an abandoned well. Her curiosity caused her to get trapped inside the well for over fifty-eight hours while the world anxiously watched a crew of dedicated rescuers attempt to free her.

On the morning of October 14, 1987, Jessica was playing with some other children in the backyard of her aunt's Midland, Texas home. While Jessica was playing, the other children removed a potted plant that had been covering the top of the well. Jessica wanted to take a closer look and see what the plant had been hiding underneath it. She sat herself down on the edge of the well and dangled her feet inside the narrow opening.

A Scary Fall

When she tried to stand up, Jessica lost her balance and fell inside. The well was 120-feet deep, but Jessica only fell around 22 feet before getting wedged inside. Her left leg dangled beneath her while her right leg got pinned up close to her chest. Jessica's forehead was stuck against the side of the well. While it was a very uncomfortable position, it kept Jessica from falling any farther.

It's not known how long it took for someone to notice her absence. But, in a short time, a crew of rescuers and citizen volunteers were feverishly working to free her. They started digging a shaft next to the well where she was trapped. A layer of extremely hard rock hampered the rescue effort.

"I don't think that I've ever drilled through anything harder than that," recalled driller Charles Boler. "You could hear her crying as we got closer. That's what kept me going because I had a two-year-old child at the time and I could identify with the family."

Between a Rock and a Hard Place

By using a water jet cutter to help them bore through the dense rock, the rescuers drilled a vertical shaft parallel to the well. Then they had to go through more solid rock to bore a five-foot-long horizontal tunnel to reach Jessica. The dense caliche, or hardpan rock, they bored through blunted the power of the diamond-tipped bits on their pneumatic drills.

The rescuers monitored Jessica by lowering a microphone into the well. They could hear Jessica alternately crying for her mother, humming, and singing. Jessica comforted herself by singing "Jesus Loves Me" and the "Winnie-the-Pooh" song. One rescuer said, "I made her mad. I've been telling her for the last twenty hours that we were coming down to get her out. I don't think she believes me."

Heat was blown into the hole to keep Jessica from shivering. She stayed warm, but she had to go without food and water while she was trapped. Doctors were worried that liquids and food could worsen any internal injuries that she may have sustained. Another concern was that trying to eat in such a tight space would cause her to choke.

Headline News

A horde of reporters, photographers, cameramen, and news outlets descended upon the rescue site. They brought news of Jessica's ordeal to millions of people throughout the world. In America, Jessica's entrapment and rescue overshadowed other major news stories like a stock market crash and First Lady Nancy Reagan undergoing cancer surgery. In Europe, German and British television stations carried live coverage of the rescue. In Japan, the rescue of Jessica was a front-page story in their major newspapers.

On Friday, October 16, Jessica was rescued. Television cameras showed a barefoot, dirty, and bruised little girl being raised from the well. Jessica's right hand was stuck to her face and her head was bandaged. She was strapped to a board. Scott Shaw, a photographer for the *Odessa American*, won a Pulitzer Prize for his photo of Jessica's rescue. CBS anchorman Dan Rather proclaimed, "Live and direct from Midland, Texas. Jessica McClure is up. She's alive. What a fighter."

Jessica was rushed to the Midland Memorial Hospital. She was dehydrated and her weight was down from twenty-one pounds to seventeen-and-a-half. There were no broken bones or internal injuries. Yet a lack blood circulating to one foot and to her forehead caused some complications. Jessica had one toe amputated and had to undergo repeated skin grafting operations and other surgeries that left many

Rescue Equipment:
The Water Jet Cutter

The rescue of Jessica McClure was greatly aided by a high-tech device known as a water jet cutter. Dr. Norman Franz, a forestry engineer, is credited with being its inventor. He began experimenting with using a high-pressure, high-speed stream of water to cut through lumber. But Dr. Franz found that it was difficult to continually maintain the high water pressure needed to do the cutting.

Then, in 1979, Dr. Mohamed Hashish improved on Dr. Franz's work by adding abrasives to the water. By doing that, Dr. Hashish found that the water jet cutter could cut through practically any material. By 1980 abrasive water jet cutters were being used to cut through glass, concrete, and steel.

The basic technology behind the tool is simple. Water flows through a pump and out of a cutting head at high rates of speed and pressure. But the water jet cutter has to be very carefully constructed. Even a slight leak can cause permanent damage to the components. The water shoots out at what's called ultra-high pressure (UHP). UHP is defined as pressure that exceeds 30,000 pounds per square inch.

The aviation and space industries were some of the first users of the water jet cutter. They found it to be perfect for cutting through high-strength materials like stainless steel and titanium. Today, some of the many industries to use it include jet engine manufacturers, tile, glass, and shipbuilding.

Another reason for the water jet cutter's widespread use and popularity is that it's an earth friendly or "green" technology. It doesn't produce any hazardous waste. When it cuts through materials like asbestos or fiberglass, it doesn't create fumes, smoke, or dust particles. The cutters use only about a half-gallon of water per minute and the water can be recycled. Still, the device does have some limitations. A water jet cutter can't cut through diamonds, tempered glass, and certain ceramics.

scars. She was in the hospital for over a month and in that time had six surgeries.

There were concerns that Jessica would also suffer permanent psychological damage. But it seems she was too young to develop any vivid or lasting memories of her ordeal. She doesn't suffer from claustrophobia, as some experts had predicted.

Life After Her Ordeal

Twenty years after her rescue, Jessica told NBC news that falling down a well "couldn't cage me then, why should it cage me now?"

For a brief time after her rescue, Jessica was a celebrity. Former Midland residents Vice President George H. W. Bush and his wife, Barbara, visited Jessica when she was hospitalized. President Ronald Reagan called her. Jessica got to throw out the first pitch at a Texas Rangers baseball game. Anonymous donors paid for her medical care and additional money was put in trust fund that she will receive when she's twenty-five years old. Her rescue also became the subject of a 1989 TV movie, *Everybody's Baby: The Rescue of Jessica McClure*.

Since then, Jessica has guarded her privacy. She stayed in the Midland area, graduated from a nearby high school, and got married. She gave birth to a son of her own in 2006. In 2002 she did a rare interview with the *Ladies Home Journal.* She insisted that she had no memory of her entrapment and rescue but did have a recurring dream in which she woke up and couldn't find her mother. Jessica added that her physical scars didn't bother her.

"I'm proud of them," Jessica said. "I have them because I survived."

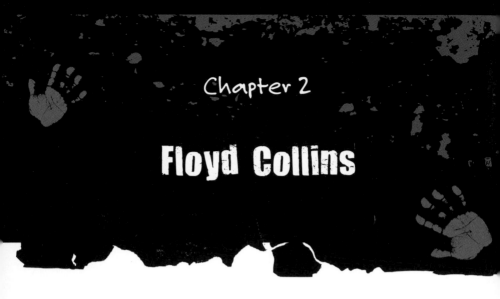

Chapter 2

Floyd Collins

Exploring caves was Floyd Collins's reason for living...and for dying. Floyd grew up in the cave country of central Kentucky. He explored his first cave when he was six and became fascinated with the subterranean (underground) world within in a world that he had discovered. Floyd dropped out of school so could spend more time caving.

Floyd's Cave

When he was in his teens, Floyd saved enough money to buy a piece of land that had a small cave. He named it Floyd's Cave and began selling stone formations from it to souvenir-seeking tourists. Later on, he found a larger cave on his family's property. Floyd and his family believed that the cave could become a big tourist attraction.

Over a period of three weeks, Floyd explored a hole in the ground that would later be known as Sand Cave. Floyd had hopes that Sand Cave would connect with nearby Mammoth Cave, a popular place to visit. Floyd had made an agreement with three farmers who owned land close to the area's main highway. If he found a cave on their land that could become a tourist attraction, they would pay to develop the cave and Floyd would get a share of the tourist proceeds.

An Ill-Advised Kick

On January 30, 1925, Floyd was exploring Sand Cave. After a few hours of wiggling and squeezing through narrow passageways, Floyd saw that his lantern was losing power. He tried to exit the cave but got trapped. While inching his way through a narrow fissure, Floyd tried kicking his way through it. One of his kicks dislodged a rock that pinned down his left ankle. When he tried kicking again, a load of silt and smaller rocks rained down on him and buried his legs.

Floyd's left arm was wedged beneath him and his right side was crammed against the cave's cold ceiling. Floyd probably tried yelling and digging his way out, before he decided to conserve his voice and energy. He was trapped fifty-five feet underground. Floyd told himself that he would be missed and that family and friends would come looking for him. That was his only hope and consolation.

Help Arrives

The following morning, a small rescue party found Floyd. They offered him words of comfort and encouragement. They also brought him coffee, sandwiches, quilts, and blankets.

They ran a lightbulb down to the passageway where Floyd was trapped. That gave him some light and a little bit of warmth.

The news of Floyd Collins's underground entrapment spread quickly. A growing pack of reporters swarmed to the rescue site. Volunteer rescuers flocked to the site along with thousands of curious spectators and scores of vendors selling sodas, hot dogs, moonshine, balloons, and other souvenirs. The National Guard was sent to the site to maintain some semblance of order.

An Uncertain Rescue

A steady rain, the circus-like atmosphere, and the unyielding and entrapping rocks that buried Floyd hampered the rescue efforts. Rescuers futilely hacked away at the rocks with a crowbar. There was ample manpower. Enthusiastic volunteer workers set a goal of digging down two feet every hour. But as the hole deepened, it became narrower. Only two workers could dig at one time and the unrelenting rain threatened to cave in the sides of the man-made shaft.

Other options were considered. Explosives, power equipment, and pneumatic drills were sent to the rescue site. But none of those were considered feasible. The slow, old-fashioned use of picks and shovels seemed to be the only safe way to free Floyd.

While the rescue efforts dragged on, there were rampant rumors about whether Floyd was dead or still alive. William "Skeets" Miller, a reporter for the *Louisville Courier-Journal* was the only one of the 150 or so reporters to actually go down into the dark, dank tunnel to interview Floyd. His riveting account of Floyd's entrapment won him a Pulitzer Prize.

Floyd's Last Words

Miller made seven trips in three days and his incredible interviews were front-page news in practically every major American newspaper. When Miller asked him if he was afraid, Floyd expressed the courage and faith that had sustained him during the ordeal:

Spelunking Safety

Although Floyd Collins was an experienced caver, he ignored two basic safety rules for exploring caves: Floyd went exploring by himself and he didn't tell anyone where he was going. If he had done either one, he would have had a much better chance of being rescued.

Caving, like all other outdoor sports, has its dangers. But following a few common sense safety procedures can minimize the dangers.

Going with a guide or a group may be the most important one to follow. If you go in a group, the ideal size is four to six cavers. That's better than having a larger group where it's harder for everyone to stay together. If you go without a guide, at least two people in your group should be experienced cavers who know their way around the cave you're exploring.

You should always let several people know you're going caving. Let them know whom you're going with, where you're going, and when you're expected to be back home. Then they can quickly report your absence if you're not home in time.

Before you begin, check your supplies to make sure that you have everything you're going to need. That includes extra batteries and bulbs to ensure that you will always have enough light. Be sure to check your food and water supplies to ensure that you've got enough for the exploration. Bring plenty of warm clothing and some good shoes to keep your feet warm and dry.

Always stay together and don't let another caver stray from the group. It's a good practice to keep the slowest caver at the front of the group. That eliminates the risk of leaving anyone behind. Even in a cave that appears to be easy to navigate, you should take frequent breaks to see how everyone in your group is doing.

Accidents often occur when the caver is careless or takes unnecessary risks.

Always take the easiest route. Instead of trying to jump over a crevice, walk around it. It takes more time, but it reduces the chances of suffering an injury or having an accident. Even a minor injury can be serious since the caver needs to be evacuated.

If someone does get too injured to make it out on their own; don't leave them alone. Send two or more people to summon help from the paramedics or police. The injured caver and the one staying with them should have a cell phone, ample food and water, clothing, and a backup lighting source like a lantern or flashlight.

Finally, if you're hopelessly lost in a cave, try not to panic and stay where your are. That will conserve your strength and energy and make it easier for rescuers to locate you. Moving around will just make you harder to find. And once again—let several people know when and where you're going caving.

"I've faced death afore, it don't frighten me none. But it's so long—so long…I begged God to send help to me."

Still, all the help that Floyd received couldn't save him. The massive rescue effort ended in failure. On February 4, the cave passage used to reach Floyd collapsed in two places. The rescuers valiantly pressed on by digging a shaft and lateral tunnel to reach Floyd. They found his lifeless body on February 17.

On April 26, Floyd was buried on his family's homestead. During the burial, the customary act of sprinkling a few clods of dirt onto the top of the casket wasn't performed. The minister who performed the ceremony later explained: "Somehow, it wouldn't have seemed appropriate in Floyd's case."

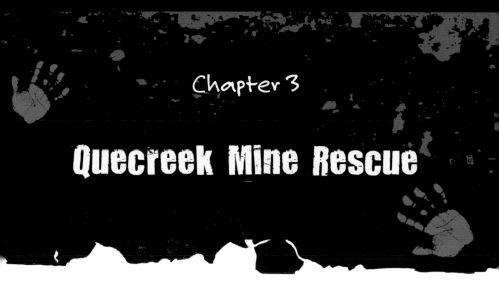

Chapter 3

Quecreek Mine Rescue

On July 24, 2002, the three o'clock evening shift began like any other day for a nine-man crew at the Quecreek Mine in Somerset County, Pennsylvania. They descended 240 feet underground into the coal mine. Soon, all of the nine miners were bent over while working in the cramped four-foot (1.2 meters) high, twelve-foot (3.6 meters) wide shaft. They worked quietly and quickly while the mining machine was noisily digging out a vein of a coal.

An Ominous Sound

The crewmen were only about two hours from finishing their shift. Suddenly, the loud grinding and boring of the machine was drowned out by a scary, unfamiliar noise. It was the sound of millions of gallons of water gushing into the shaft through a six-foot gash. The machine had cut into an abandoned mine that was filled with water. It was like poking a hole through a huge dam.

Fifty million gallons of chilly 55-degree water rapidly poured into their small underground chamber. The miners moved as quickly as possible toward the elevator that might have led them to safety. But already, the water was rushing in way too fast. In a short time, it was up to their waists. They climbed on top of a conveyor belt and began looking for an exit.

Warning Call

Before they became trapped, a miner used the mine's phone system to warn another crew of the impending danger. That crew was able to safely exit the mine and alert authorities to the catastrophe. Within minutes, a rescue operation was underway.

Bob Long was one of the first people notified. Long had access to a Global Positioning System (GPS) that could pinpoint the location of the miners. Once Long found the miners' exact location, the rescuers could dig holes for getting air to them and for bringing them above ground.

"The key question was, 'Where exactly were these

guys?'" Long recalled. "And we were going to get them out by drilling a rescue shaft, where exactly do we drill it?"

Long started out by looking at some maps of the mine. That gave him information on the slope of the mine and helped him determine where the high ground was. That's where the miners were likeliest to go. Then, he spent about ninety minutes entering data into the GPS equipment and staking out the area. At around 1:15 A.M., Thursday, Long picked an exact spot. He pounded a stake into the ground and a crew began drilling.

Holding Back the Flood

When the drilling began, the nine miners were building a barricade of concrete blocks to hold back the water. Barricading themselves in would keep the water away for a few hours and allow them to conserve body heat. But they were working under terribly adverse conditions. The air around them was heavy and hot because the water had knocked out the ventilation system. Some of the miners were starting to feel light-headed.

Their barricade didn't hold. Water came surging in around it and then one section fell over. As bad as things were, the miners still stubbornly clung to their hopes of getting out alive.

Their spirits were raised when they heard the sound of a powerful drill boring through the ground above them. The crew's foreman, Randy Fogle, easily identified the sound and what it meant.

"I knew from how fast it was coming down that it wasn't a rescue hole," Fogle recalled. "I knew that it was communications or air. You're not going to drill that fast if it's a rescue hole."

After about seven hours of drilling, a 6-inch (15-centimeter) pipe reached the mine tunnel. A member of the rescue crew hit the pipe with a sledgehammer and waited for a response. The miners heard the noise and followed it to the pipe. They responded by tapping on the pipe nine times. That was a signal that all nine miners were still alive.

As the fresh air rushed down the pipe, the water level was slowly sinking. Powerful diesel pumps were removing an estimated 20,000 gallons (91,000 liters) of liquid a minute from the mine. But just when it seemed like operations were going smoothly, the rescue team suffered a serious setback early Friday morning.

Starting Over

The drilling of the escape hole had come to an abrupt halt because the thick metal drill bit got stuck in the rocky ground and snapped off. A new bit quickly arrived by helicopter, but it took hours to retrieve the old bit, which was buried one hundred feet deep. A second drilling rig was brought in and they began digging a second rescue hole.

Drilling was delayed for around eighteen hours. During that time, the miners could only communicate by tapping on the pipe. The miners thought about their families and loved ones. In unison, they recited the Lord's Prayer. Then they resumed their waiting and hoping.

Rescue Crew Reaches the Miners

Around 10:15 P.M., Saturday, the drill bit broke through into the chamber where the miners were huddled together. About an hour later, the rescue workers confirmed that they made contact with the miners via a cell phone lowered into the first rescue shaft. Shortly before one o'clock in the morning on Sunday, Randy Fogle became the first of the miners to emerge from the rescue shaft. By 2:45 A.M., all nine

Global Positioning System

When the Quecreek Mine rescue occurred, GPS systems weren't nearly as widely used as they are today. They weren't a high-tech tool that you would find in a car or on a cell phone. Today, anyone can buy a pocket-sized GPS receiver for less than a hundred dollars.

Usually, when people talk about a GPS they mean a GPS receiver. Actually, the Global Positioning System refers to a network of twenty-four Earth-orbiting satellites called Navstars. The Navstars are used to send signals to a GPS receiver. The receiver's job is to locate four or more of these Navstars, calculate the distance to each one, and use that data to deduce the exact location of the receiver.

Each Navstar signal gives the exact location of the satellite that sent it and the time it took for the receiver to get the signal. The receiver "knows" that it's located somewhere on the surface of an imaginary circle. Then it determines the sizes of several circles, one for each Navstar. The receiver's location is the spot on the earth's surface where the circles intersect.

Most commercial GPS receivers can determine their location within a range of ten meters (thirty-three feet). A technique called carrier phase GPS can be accurate to within one centimeter (0.4 inch).

After the Quecreek miners were rescued, Bob Long said that he had great faith in the accuracy of the technology. It was simply a matter of knowing how to use it.

"I bet nine lives on GPS," Long told a writer. "Just trust the unit. It knows what to do."

miners were safely above ground. They were wet, hungry, and fatigued, but delighted to be alive.

The rescued miners received immediate medical attention and all nine made full recoveries from their seventy-seven-hour ordeal. Randy Fogle was the only one of the miners to return to working underground.

About a year after the near-fatal accident at the Quecreek mine, the Pennsylvania Department of Environmental Regulation issued a fifty-two-page report that blamed the disaster on the use of outdated maps. The detailed report made twenty-six specific recommendations for improving coal mine safety. Since then, safety has improved, but coal mining is still a dirty and dangerous job.

Chapter 4

Elandsrand Mine Rescue

W hat could have been the world's worst mining disaster became the world's biggest underground rescue.

On October 4, 1987, 3,200 gold miners were working 1.4 miles underground at the Elandsrand gold mine in South Africa. Around ten o'clock in the morning, the workers became trapped when a fifty-foot section of a compressed air pipe broke loose and tumbled into the mine's main elevator shaft. The falling pipe severely damaged the shaft's steel frame and severed the electrical lines that powered the elevator.

Slowly but Surely

Fortunately, there was a smaller elevator nearby that was still working. It was normally used for removing debris and hauling equipment. The rescue was a long, slow process because the smaller elevator could only transport seventy to seventy-five miners at a time. Usually, the smaller elevator took only three minutes to reach the mine entrance. But it operated at a much slower speed during the rescue because of problems with the electrical power.

The successful rescue took somewhere between thirty-eight and forty hours. The trapped miners—men and women—were confined to a cramped space where the temperatures ranged from 86 to 104 degrees Fahrenheit. Many of the miners were crying, believing they would die in the underground mine. One of the rescued miners said that the biggest discomfort wasn't the darkness, the heat, or the anxiety. It was the overwhelming stench of over three thousand profusely sweating people in a small, confined space.

Some Second Guessing

The response and rescue by the mine's owners, the Harmony Gold Mining Company, brought them both praise and criticism. They were praised for rescuing 3,200 miners without the loss of any lives. The criticism came from the company withholding the news of a potential disaster. They failed to promptly inform both government officials and the general public of the accident and near disaster.

There are differing accounts of when the news of the accident and near disaster was first reported. A story in *The New York Times* said that Harmony announced the accident on Wednesday evening, around ten hours after the miners became trapped. Lizelle du Toit, a company spokeswoman said that the company waited because it initially believed that the workers would be brought out quickly.

Be that as it may, the newspaper *China Daily* reported that the National Union of Mineworkers was the first to report the news of the miners' perilous situation. How and when the union learned of the accident wasn't mentioned. The newspaper said the union reported the news fifteen hours after the accident occurred. There seems to be a general agreement that neither source informed any South African government officials. It was reported that the officials learned about the accident by watching the late evening news.

"You cannot hide 3,000 people who are trapped underground," said Buyelwa Sonjica, the South African government's minister for minerals and energy. "I find it very queer, strange that they did that. As to whether they were covering it up it is difficult to tell at this point."

Everyone Gets Out Alive

Shortly before nine o'clock Thursday night, the final group of forty-five dusty, dirty, and dazed miners stepped off of the backup elevator to be greeted by family and friends. Amazingly, there was only one reported health problem—a miner who was treated for dehydration. One other miner fell down while waiting to be rescued and was carried out on a stretcher.

Miner Richman Maneli was relieved to be out. "It has been thirty hours of suffering. We had no food, no water, and we are exhausted."

In the aftermath of the near disaster and incredible rescue, Minerals and Energy Minister Sonjica closed the mine for six weeks as a precaution. She said, "I wouldn't call it a crisis given that mining is risky in its nature, so incidents of this kind will occur, but I still think there is room for improvement to reduce accidents in the mines."

Immediately after the incident, the National Union of Mineworkers was threatening to strike. Spokesman Lesiba Seshoka said, "An industry-wide strike is now coming under serious consideration. We have given

Gold Mining Deaths

In gold mining, the deeper you dig, the more dangerous it becomes. South Africa has the deepest gold mines, as well as the most gold mining related deaths. According to a recent estimate, in the past hundred years over 54,000 gold miners have died while working in South African mines.

In 1904 the South African government began keeping records of gold mining fatalities. During that year 382 deaths were reported and recorded.

The worst gold mining accident in recent history occurred in 1995 when 105 miners were killed. They were riding in a mine elevator when a runaway ore train severed the cable supporting the elevator. The doomed miners fell more than two kilometers (1.25 miles) before the elevator crashed to the bottom of the mine.

In 2007, the year of the Elandsrand rescue, the annual death toll rose to 221 miners. As a result, the South African government began shutting down most of the mines that reported any fatal accidents. That reduced the death toll from 209 in 2006 to 170 in 2007.

But even with more stringent safety standards, deaths occur because the rising price of gold has caused outlaw mining companies and miners to explore abandoned mines. Outlaw miners will break through concrete seals on closed shafts to try to mine any remaining gold. In June 2009 there were reports that sixty-one miners died from a fire in an abandoned mine. Additional accidents have reportedly killed an estimated twenty illegal miners in 2009.

In summer 2009 the price of gold rose to over $1,000 an ounce. Gold deposits that were once considered too impure or too deep to mine are now thought to be worth the costs and the risks. The AngloGold Ashanti mining firm currently has the world's deepest gold mine, the TauTona or "Great Lion" mine west of Johannesburg, South Africa. It announced plans to extend the mine to 2.4 miles (3.9 kilometers) underground.

Another South African company has said that it's going to go even deeper. The Gold Fields Ltd. company plans to set a new world record by extending its Driefontein mine 2.5 miles (4 kilometers) underground. The corporation is hoping to extract an estimated 8.5 million ounces of gold. At over $1,000 an ounce, that's an estimated value of over $8.5 billion.

When there are great rewards, mining companies are inclined to take great risks. The loss of lives is considered part of the cost of doing business.

them the opportunity to improve their safety targets, but they have not." After all was said and done, the strike did not take place.

During the time that the mine was closed, the shaft was repaired and the accident was investigated. Yet there were no reports of Harmony being fined or even officially reprimanded for the accident or for their tardiness in reporting it to government officials.

Chapter 5

Wesley Autrey

American author and essayist Ralph Waldo Emerson defined what a hero is by writing, "A hero is no braver than an ordinary man, but he is braver five minutes longer."

Construction worker Wesley Autrey's few minutes of bravery saved a fellow New Yorker from a certain death. His heroic underground rescue didn't occur in a cave or a coal mine. It happened beneath the bustling streets and sidewalks of one of the world's largest cities.

Sudden Crisis

On the afternoon of January 2, 2007, Autrey and his two young daughters were standing on a Manhattan subway platform below the intersection of 137th Street and Broadway. A twenty-year-old college student,

Cameron Hollopeter, was quietly standing nearby. Suddenly, Hollopeter collapsed and began writhing on the platform. Autrey could see that he was in the throes of a seizure.

Autrey acted quickly. He used a pen to keep Hollopeter from getting his tongue stuck in his throat. The seizure subsided, and for a few moments it seemed like everything would be okay. But when Hollopeter stood up, he stumbled to the edge of the platform and fell onto the subway tracks between the two rails.

Bad Situation Gets Worse

While Hollopeter was laying helplessly on the tracks, Autrey saw the lights of an oncoming subway car.

"I had to make a split decision," Autrey said.

He left his daughters on the platform while he jumped off. Autrey would later say that his choices were trying to save Hollopeter or letting his two daughters watch someone get run over by a subway train. He wanted to pull Hollopeter off the tracks, but he quickly realized there wasn't enough time. He threw himself on Hollopeter's body and pressed down on him. Autrey tried to get Hollopeter to lie still, but he kept thrashing around and struggling. Autrey ordered him to freeze by telling him: "Don't move! Or one of us is going to lose a leg."

While they lay in a drainage trench, the five subway cars roared and rolled a few inches above them. After the cars passed over them, Autrey's blue knit cap was smudged with grease.

Sigh of Relief

In spite of the din of the passing cars, Autrey could hear the screams of onlookers. Then, he heard their cheers and applause. When it got quiet, Autrey yelled up to them.

"We're okay down here," Autrey yelled, "but I've got two daughters up there. Let them know their father's okay."

After waiting twenty minutes, Autrey and Hollopeter were freed by subway workers when the power to the subway's high voltage third rail was shut off. Then, they were taken to a local hospital. Hollopeter had only a few bumps and bruises. Autrey refused any medical assistance. He simply said that there wasn't anything wrong with him.

The day after the rescue, news of Autrey's heroic act was widely reported in newspapers and television. Before the day ended, he was being flooded with gifts

Subway Safety

In the midst of a seizure, Cameron Hollopeter couldn't avoid falling off of a subway platform. But in most cases you can avoid it by remembering to follow a few simple safety rules. Remembering these rules can ensure your safety when you're waiting to get on the subway.

The farther you stand back from the platform's edge, the less likely you are to fall onto the tracks. In New York City, the platform's edge is clearly marked with a yellow strip. Even if you're in a hurry to board the train, remember to stand behind the strip.

Some of the newer subway systems have made their platforms safer by installing safety shields. The shields have doors on them that line up with the car doors when the train stops. They've become more common-place in Asia where people have committed suicide by jumping on the tracks.

Other subway systems have considered the use of cameras that would allow drivers to see if a person or some other obstruction is in their path. That's less expensive than installing screens.

Most subway-related accidents don't occur on the platforms or the tracks; they occur on the stairways. Trips, slips, and falls occur when riders get in a hurry to catch the train. Even if you're running late, slow down when you're on the stairs and hold on to the handrail. If you miss your ride there will always be another one stopping at the platform later on.

If you drop something on the tracks, don't try to retrieve it. The third rail of the subway tracks has six hundred volts of live electricity coursing through it, so it's not worth the risk. You can retrieve the item by going to the station booth and telling the agent you dropped something.

Once you board the subway car, make sure personal items like backpacks, packages, and umbrellas are clear of the closing doors. When you're inside of a moving car, never ride between the cars, or lean against the doors. If you're standing, keep your balance by holding on to one of straps or bars.

The subway is a safe, reliable and affordable way of getting around a big city. It becomes dangerous when riders take unnecessary risks.

and phone calls from well-wishers. Among his many gifts were a $10,000 check from Donald Trump, a free trip to Disney World for himself and his daughters, and a new Jeep Patriot. Autrey also received New York City's top award for civic achievement, the Bronze Medal, from Mayor Michael Bloomberg. Mayor Bloomberg called Autrey "… a great man who makes us all proud to be New Yorkers."

National Hero

Later that month, Autrey and his daughters were the special guests of President George W. Bush when he presented his 2007 State of the Union Address. The president recounted the story of Autrey's unselfishness and bravery, then added: "There is something wonderful about a country that produces a brave and humble man like Wesley Autrey."

TIME magazine even included Autrey in its 2007 list of the most influential people in the world. Business tycoon Donald Trump wrote, "Autrey automatically became an influential person by merit of his extaordinary behavior, which I hope will encourage and inspire other people to follow his example."

While he enjoyed the praise and attention, Autrey

maintained that he didn't do anything spectacular or extraordinary.

"I don't feel like I did something spectacular; I just saw someone who needed help," Autrey said. "I did what I felt was right."

abrasive—Any material or substance used for grinding or polishing.

catastrophe—A sudden, violent disturbance.

caliche—Hard crust of calcium carbonate, a stone-like mineral that forms over the soil in dry regions. Caliche is very hard to break through.

claustrophobia—An abnormal fear of being in an enclosed place.

consolation—Something that comforts someone or lessens their disappointment.

deduce—To determine.

dehydration—The loss of bodily fluids or water.

extraordinary—Exceptional to a high degree.

fissure—A narrow opening.

moonshine—Illegally manufactured corn liquor.

pneumatic drill—A drill powered by air pressure.

rampant—Unchecked and widespread.

riveting—Firmly holding someone's attention.

seizure—A sudden spasm or convulsion of the body.

semblance—A resemblance or appearance of something that's not actually occurring.

stench—A strong, foul odor.

stringent—Strict or exacting.

subterranean—Existing or operating below the surface of the earth, underground.

throes—Conditions of agonizing effort or struggle.

unison—Two or more people reciting the same words at the same time.

via—By means of.

vein—A lode or deposit of mined coal or ore.

writhing—To twist or squirm as in pain.

More Books You'll Like

Brimner, Larry Dane. *Subway: The Story of Tunnels, Tubes, and Tracks*. Honesdale, Pa.: Boyds Mills Press, 2004.

Clark, Domini. *South Africa: The Land*. New York: Crabtree Pub. Co., 2008.

Matthews, Sheelagh. *Mining*. Calgary, AB, Canada: Weigl Educational Publishers, 2007.

Shea, George. *Amazing Rescues*. New York: Random House, 2003.

Skog, Jason. *The Monongah Mining Disaster*. Mankato, Minn.: Compass Point Books, 2008.

Swart, Peter K. *Caving: The Essential Guide to Equipment and Techniques*. Mechanicsburg, Pa.: Stackpole Books, 2002.

Todd, Anne M. *Caving Adventures*. Mankato, Minn.: Capstone, 2002.

Find Out More

Caving Safety & Techniques from the National Speleological Society

<http://www.caves.org/safety/safety.shtml>

"How Can Water Cut Through Steel?" from HowStuffWorks.com

<http://science.howstuffworks.com/question553.htm>

"Man Is Rescued by Stranger on Subway Tracks"

<http://www.nytimes.com/2007/01/03/nyregion/03life.html?_r=1&pagewanted=print>

Mine Safety and Health Administration's (MSHA) Kid's Page from the Department of Labor

<http://www.msha.gov/kids/kidshp.htm>

Subway Safety from *Safety Issues* magazine

<http://www.safetyissues.com/magazine/2002/5/SubwaySafety/SubwaySafety.htm>

"20 Years Later, Baby Jessica Lives Quietly in Tex."

<http://today.msnbc.msn.com/id/19165433/>

Index

TRUE MOUNTAIN RESCUE STORIES

Shocking and triumphant true accounts of railroad wrecks, plane and helicopter crashes, and mountaineers who nearly met their maker are featured in this collection.

ISBN: 978-0-7660-3572-7

TRUE OCEAN RESCUE STORIES

A naval ship lost in battle, a vessel wrecked by an iceberg, and even a surfer rescued by a family of dolphins are some of the exciting tales of struggle and survival that will keep you on the edge of your seat.

ISBN: 978-0-7760-3665-9

TRUE UNDERGROUND RESCUE STORIES

The harrowing tales of a baby trapped in a well, a man looking for caves in Kentucky, coal miners and gold miners put in deadly predicaments, and a man rescuing another from an oncoming subway train.

ISBN: 978-0-7660-3676-5

TRUE WILDERNESS RESCUE STORIES

Read about thrilling rescues that took place in the wild, such as how a person was saved from a burning forest fire, and how a group of friends was rescued by their dog.

ISBN: 978-0-7660-3666-6